A Pocket Guide to

Hiking
Mount Desert
Island

Earl D. Brechlin

Maps by Ruth Ann Hill

DOWN EAST BOOKS, Camden, Maine

67578

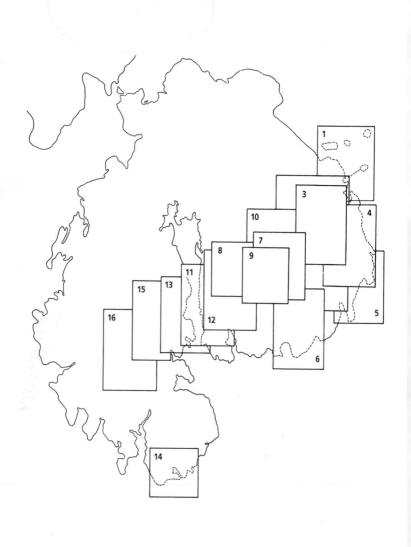

Contents

This guide is dedicated to the hardworking men and women who share their love of Mt. Desert with all of us by toiling to maintain the island's trails and paths. From seasonal trail crews employed by the National Park Service and Friends of Acadia, to volunteers working as groups and individuals, we owe them our deepest respect and gratitude.

Copyright © 1996 by Earl D. Brechlin
ISBN 0-89272-356-4
Library of Congress Catalog Card No. 95-71936
Cover photograph by Alan Nyiri
Author photograph by Peter Travers
Color separation by Roxmont Graphics
Printed and bound at Capital City Press

9   8   7   6   5   4   3   2   1

DOWN EAST BOOKS, CAMDEN, ME 04843

Introduction

More than 100 years ago when the first "rusticators," inspired by the paintings of Thomas Cole and others of the Hudson River School, discovered Mount Desert Island, hiking—walking as it was called then—was the primary form of recreational and social activity. Leisurely all-day walks with friends and a picnic lunch were the norm, with plenty of stops to discuss the literature and politics of the day.

There were no auto roads through Acadia National Park. Indeed, until 1917 no cars were allowed on Mount Desert Island, and Acadia National Park itself did not exist in national monument form until 1916, and did not take the name Acadia until 1929.

As the popularity of the island increased, so-called Village Improvement Societies were formed in each town. Along with civic improvements such as parks and safer water supplies, they worked with a group called the Hancock County Trustees for Public Reservations, and with George B. Dorr, the park's first superintendent, to create the network of hiking trails we enjoy today.

It is said that at the peak of this activity, more than 250 miles of maintained hiking trails crisscrossed Acadia's barren summits and ran down the steep-sided valleys and along the rocky shore. Each trail is unique in the terrain it traverses, the views it offers, and in the tale it tells of the island's geologic, ecologic, and human history.

Unlike anywhere else in New England, the trails on Mount Desert Island provide views quickly as they ascend to open alpine summits. Only here, where climate zones overlap, can so many different types of flora and fauna be found so close together.

While not big by the standards of the White Mountains to the west and lofty, mile-high Katahdin to the north, Acadia's mountains offer unsurpassed 360-degree panoramas.

Although only half the original 250 miles of trails are still mapped and cared for, hiking along a quiet lake shore, through the misty silence of the deep forest, or across open summits swept by brisk winds, remains one of the prime recreational activities and one of the few ways to discover the true beauty and majesty of Mount Desert Island, much as those first visitors did so long ago.

Protecting the Resource

At just over 34,000 acres, Acadia is one of the smallest national parks. Much of the activity associated with nearly three million annual visitors is concentrated on the eastern side of Mount Desert Island. Because of this intensive use, visitors must take it upon themselves to be wise stewards of the area's natural beauty.

Pack it in, pack it out—Take nothing but photographs and leave nothing but footprints. If you see some litter on the trail, help out by picking it up and packing it out yourself.

Stay on the trail—Especially on high open ridges, the sub-alpine vegetation is extremely sensitive to damage by walkers. Stay on the trail and on bare rock whenever possible. In muddy areas, stay on the rough log "bog walks."

Preserve vegetation—Don't break branches or trample plants unnecessarily. Picking of wild blueberries and other fruits for personal consumption is allowed in Acadia National Park.

Leave wildlife alone—Spotting an animal in the wild is one of the real thrills of hiking. Don't harass the animals or offer them food. Once animals have become imprinted with the notion of people as a source of food, they drop their natural fear of humans. This can cause them great harm later and can also affect their ability to utilize natural food sources.

Pets—All pets in Acadia National Park must remain on leashes. Owners can be summonsed for unleashed pets.

Fire—Fires are allowed only in designated campgrounds and picnic areas. If you want a hot beverage or soup while hiking, pack it in a thermos or bring a small, portable backpacking stove along.

Camping—Camping is allowed only in the Blackwoods Campground and the Seawall Campground in the park and in private campgrounds nearby. Rangers conduct regular backcountry patrols, and from time to time even use night-vision equipment to catch scofflaws.

Swimming—Many of the larger lakes on Mount Desert Island are public water supplies for area towns. Eagle Lake, Jordan Pond,

Upper and Lower Hadlock Ponds, and portions of Long Pond in Southwest Harbor are all have restrictions against swimming, wading, or allowing pets to make contact with the water.

User Rules—Bicycles and horses are banned from all hiking trails. Some restrictions apply concerning horse and bicycle use on the carriage road system. For example, horses are not allowed on the carriage road around Witch Hole Pond or on the west side of Eagle Lake. Bicycles are banned on the Rockefeller-owned carriage roads in Seal Harbor. When in doubt, check with park officials. Trail courtesy rules call for bicyclists to yield to walkers and horses and for hikers to yield to horses.

Private Property—Throughout the park are sprinkled "inholdings"—areas of private property surrounded by government land. Some parts of the island, such as the land and paths around Little Long Pond in Seal Harbor, are private property, yet abut the park and are open to the public. Many other areas, such as the Shore Path in Bar Harbor and portions of Bar Island, are also privately owned. Always respect private property rights, and never trespass.

Respect Solitude—One of the hardest things to achieve in our modern world is solitude. While no one can lay claim to any part of the park as his or her own, we should all nonetheless respect peoples' privacy in the wild. Don't crowd other visitors. Don't hog the area around summit cairns or signs; allow others to also savor the moment of reaching the top.

You Can Help

The nonprofit group Friends of Acadia, in cooperation with the National Park Service, schedules regular trail maintenance work all summer. Check local publications for dates and times. Contact FOA at (207) 288-3340 or Acadia National Park at (207) 288-3338 for information on how you or your community group can help by volunteering to care for Acadia's trails.

Heading Out

Proper preparation for a day in the wild means being prepared for every eventuality. With so many to choose from, it is easy to select a route for your individual fitness level and the abilities of those in your party. Take it slowly; there is plenty of time. If you set out to "just do it," you are missing the point and won't get to savor much of what Acadia has to offer.

As Mark Twain once said of all weather in New England, "If you don't like it, wait a minute; it'll change." That goes double for Mount Desert Island, where not only does the weather change several times in a day but where weather conditions can vary greatly depending on one's altitude and proximity to the ocean. It is not unusual for it to be sunny in Bar Harbor while it is raining at Jordan Pond and Ocean Drive is socked in with pea-soup fog.

Daylight fades quickly in autumn, so make sure you have plenty of time to complete your walk before dark. It doesn't hurt to put a small flashlight in your daypack along with other essentials.

Studies have shown that the average temperature drops a degree or two for each 300- to 400-foot elevation gain. Add a steady wind, and most summits are markedly cooler than the surrounding lowlands.

Clothing

Even on the hottest days, be sure to pack a wind- and waterproof jacket. A hiker soaked in a passing shower and then buffeted by high winds can succumb to hypothermia, the sometimes deadly lowering of the body's core temperature, even when the mercury is above 60 degrees. A large percentage of body heat is lost through the head. Packing a hat is also a good idea. A disposable space blanket is also a popular pack item.

Proper footwear is vital. Many trails traverse slippery ledges that become treacherous after a rain. In some areas the dark algae that cover the rock surfaces are particularly slippery after rains. A good, solid, hard-soled boot that provides ankle support is vital. Sneakers or sports sandals offer little protection to the bottoms of feet as you leap from boulder to boulder on some trails. Sections of trails with iron ladder rungs on cliff faces are also difficult in soft footwear.

To help prevent blisters, wear a polypropylene undersock under a heavy boot sock. The inner sock will help wick moisture away from your feet, while the outer layer will reduce abrasion. A small piece of moleskin foam tucked into your first aid kit is invaluable for covering hot spots before they develop into blisters.

Water

Acadia is laced with scores of brooks and numerous large lakes, and one of the real treats of hiking through the backcountry is a refreshing drink from a mountain stream. Still, bring some water with you on a hike, as even the most reliable mountain springs can go dry in high summer. Few pollutants threaten the pristine quality of Mount Desert Island's water, although some evidence of Giardia—a naturally occurring parasite which can cause serious intestinal problems known as "beaver fever"—has been detected. The chance of contracting this problem, even when drinking unfiltered water is small, but officials in all recreational areas advise filtering or treating water before consumption. If the choice is between a powerful thirst and an unfiltered yet clear-running source, by all means drink up.

Alcoholic beverages and most sodas only seem to quench your thirst, and actually act as diuretics. They end up increasing your body's need for water.

Finding the Trail

Most trails in Acadia National Park are clearly marked on the ground and show up well on the many maps that are available.

Trailheads in Acadia are marked with lettered signs carved into wooden posts. Blue paint blazes on bare ledge, stone cairns, and metal markers fastened to trees help lead the way when the worn footpath or evidence of brush cutting is less apparent.

Trail intersections are marked with carved wooden signs on posts giving directions and distances. Occasionally some signs may be missing, so follow the map carefully as you walk.

If you lose the trail, return to the last obvious marker and have a member of your party fan out to find the next one before proceeding. This is especially important on the steeper trails such as the Precipice, where switchbacks are plentiful. So many people take wrong turns at some spots that this creates false trails, which fade quickly or stop abruptly. Piles of logs or rocks are often used by trail crews to block passage on false or closed trails. Hikers sometimes spot the remains of abandoned paths called "ghost trails." Be careful not be confused by these, or by illegal trails created by "trail phantoms." If you notice a fresh, unmapped trail or trail workers not sporting uniforms, clothing, or hats identifying them as volunteers, notify rangers immediately.

If you do become disoriented remember that most ridge lines on Mount Desert Island run in a north-south direction. Most ridges have trails that can easily be followed to safety. Bushwhacking off the trail, particularly in an east or west direction, can be very hazardous. Even a map with 50-foot contour lines does not show a lot of deadly 40-foot drops!

Stick together, or at least make arrangements to regroup members of your party at major intersections or summits, and take a head count before proceeding.

Scores of people become separated from their groups or are reported overdue in Acadia each year. Most are quickly located by park rangers or members of the volunteer Mount Desert Island Search and Rescue Group.

If hiking alone, be sure to leave a note detailing your route and the time of your expected return. That way, should you have a problem on the trail, someone will be able to summon assistance.

If darkness falls and you have not found your way, stay put. Help will come. Most of the serious injuries from falls involving lost hikers in Acadia have occurred after dark.

Other Concerns

Falls—Falls are the leading cause of injury in Acadia National Park, although more are recorded on the concrete path around Cadillac Mountain's summit and on the path along Ocean Drive than on backcountry trails. While several hikers do require technical evacuation during the typical summer season, injuries are seldom life-threatening. Most fatalities occur when individuals stray off the marked trails.

Insects—Especially from mid-May through early June, biting blackflies can make any walk in the forest a miserable experience. On any damp day without a breeze, mosquitoes can also be a problem, particularly in heavily vegetated areas. Later in the season, moose flies and deer flies may be bothersome.

Commercial repellents containing DEET seem to work best, although formulas containing the highest percentage of the chemical can damage plastic surfaces if they get onto cameras and binoculars. Natural repellents are also available, as are brands formulated especially for children.

Lyme Disease—Some deer ticks found on Mount Desert Island show evidence of debilitating Lyme disease, so general tick precautions are in order. Avoid brushy and grassy areas, and check yourself carefully for ticks after each excursion. Ticks do not attach themselves immediately, so early detection is important. If you find a tick, follow standard first aid recommendations for removal.

Lyme disease often, but not always, gives itself away with the appearance of a red rash, often in a ring around the tick-bite site. The disease's serious symptoms, which may include heart, breathing, and arthritis-like problems, may not appear until much later.

Early detection makes treatment easy. In later stages, Lyme disease is difficult to treat. Tests are available, so if in doubt contact a physician.

Sunburn—Forgetting to use sunblock while hiking or basking in the sun along the shore has ruined more vacations that any other affliction. Use of a lotion with an SPF of 15 or higher is critical during prime sunburn time between the hours of 10 a.m. and 2 p.m.

Fire—In 1947 a devastating forest fire swept across Mount Desert Island, burning thousands of acres and destroying more than 100 homes. When fire dangers rise, traditionally in late summer and early fall, park officials will sometimes ban smoking on the trails. Use all smoking materials carefully. Field strip all cigarettes and pack out the butts.

Mount Desert Island

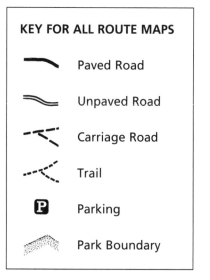

KEY FOR ALL ROUTE MAPS

Paved Road

Unpaved Road

Carriage Road

Trail

P Parking

Park Boundary

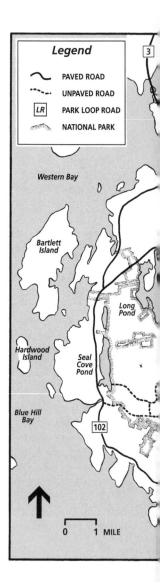

Legend

~ PAVED ROAD

----- UNPAVED ROAD

LR PARK LOOP ROAD

NATIONAL PARK

3

Western Bay

Bartlett Island

Long Pond

Hardwood Island

Seal Cove Pond

Blue Hill Bay

102

0   1 MILE

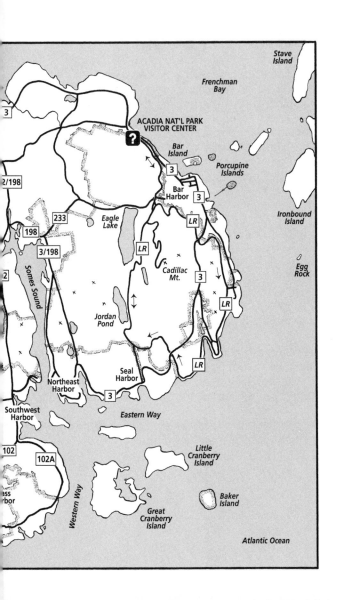

Stave
Island

Frenchman
Bay

ACADIA NAT'L PARK
VISITOR CENTER

?

Bar
Island

Porcupine
Islands

3

Bar
Harbor

3

Ironbound
Island

3

2/198

233

Eagle
Lake

198

LR

3/198

LR

Egg
Rock

2

Somes Sound

Cadillac
Mt.

3

LR

Jordan
Pond

LR

Northeast
Harbor

Seal
Harbor

LR

Southwest
Harbor

3

Eastern Way

102

102A

Little
Cranberry
Island

ass
rbor

Western Way

Baker
Island

Great
Cranberry
Island

Atlantic Ocean

How to Use This Book

The hikes profiled here are grouped geographically. All the hikes in a given chapter appear on the chapter map. The sketch map accompanying the table of contents indicates the area shown in each map. On pages 12 and 13 are a map of the entire island and a key to symbols used in the hiking route maps.

Notice that suggested times have not been included. Every hiker is different, with those in great shape being able to make several miles per hour in mountainous terrain, while those who prefer a slower pace may make only one mile per hour. Review any planned trip with your condition, the weather, the length of the trail, elevation gain, and difficulty all in mind before you leave. When in doubt, leave yourself extra time so there is no need to rush.

For some of the larger mountains, such as Cadillac, several trails may be described. A level of difficulty is indicated for each hike. The following ratings for Acadia's trails closely follow those established by the National Park Service:

Easy—Fairly level ground, small up- and downhill sections, good footing.

Moderate—Uneven ground, some steep uphills with loose rock or soil. Attention to foot placement necessary.

Strenuous—Steady climbs and descents. Long uphill stretches with careful attention needed to foot placement. Some use of hands.

Ladder—Iron rungs or handrails on some sections. Steep drop–offs. Necessary use of hands. Very difficult.

1. Bar Harbor Village

Bar Harbor Shore Path   *(Easy)*

For more than a century the Shore Path in Bar Harbor has attracted strollers with its ocean views and constant cool breezes. Maintained by the Village Improvement Association, it is located on private land open to the public through the graciousness of the owners. Please remember this and respect their privacy.

The path begins on the east side of the town pier and curves along the town beach and past the Bar Harbor Inn. The main building here, which houses the Reading Room Restaurant and Gatsby's Terrace, was built as a club during Prohibition as a place for wealthy summer residents to enjoy a discreet libation.

Just past the inn property, the path skirts the shore along Grant's Park, also known as Albert's Meadow. The park is open from dawn to dusk and is an excellent spot for a picnic, or as a place to simply sit and watch the comings and goings when one of the more than 40 oceangoing cruise ships (such as the *Queen Elizabeth 2*) that visit Frenchman Bay each year is anchored nearby.

The remainder of the 0.75-mile path remains much as it was long ago, as it skirts the front of many of the remaining mansions from the town's golden age. Several have been converted into spectacular inns.

As you walk, imagine the summer family that owned the Hope Diamond, their house now gone. Local residents remember it was not uncommon for the children to play with the priceless jewel—which is now safe in the Smithsonian in Washington D.C.—on the front lawn!

During the day, lobstermen can be seen working in their boats just offshore. Seabirds can be seen, and occasionally porpoises can be spotted frolicking in the bay.

Off to the southeast lies the Bar Harbor breakwater, built by the U.S. Army Corps of Engineers in 1901. Never completed, it is 100

MAP 1: BAR HARBOR VILLAGE

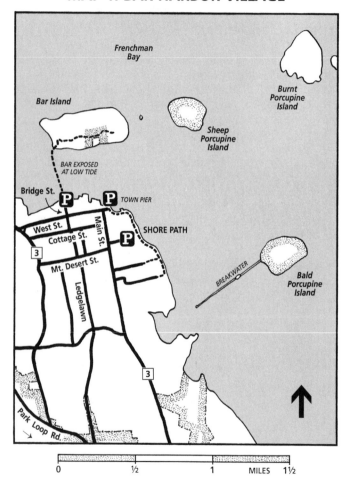

feet wide at its base and rises 60 feet from the ocean bottom.

A connecting path turns right, off the shore path, and connects with Hancock Street for a quick return to town. A little farther on, the shore path ends with a right turn up a path that ends on Wayman Lane. A right turn at the end of either of these streets will return you quickly to town.

Bar Island   *(Easy)*

Connected to the village at low tide by a wide gravel and mud bar that is covered in places by mussel beds, Bar Island is an oasis of quietude just a few hundred yards from one of the busiest tourist destinations on the East Coast.

Because of the area's sweeping tides, which average 12 feet, Bar Island is only accessible two times daily. Depending on weather conditions the bar is revealed for from about one hour before low tide to one hour after. *Watch the tide and your watch carefully!* Trying to cross while the tide is coming in is very dangerous. If you miss the tide, you will have a long wait. Consult local tide tables before going on this walk.

Although vehicles sometimes drive over the bar, you really need to walk the half mile across to truly appreciate this rare geologic feature. There are places to park on the northern end of Bridge Street where the bar begins.

Especially on a foggy day, the beauty of the bar's openness is hard to beat. There are not too many places where you can walk along the ocean bottom twice a day.

Once you're up off the rock-strewn shore, the character of this hardwood-covered island changes. There is a large field in the island's interior and a poorly marked trail to the tall, treeless knob on the eastern end. From there you have spectacular views of the village of Bar Harbor and the mountains beyond.

At one time, Bar Island was home to several families who had farms, gardens, boatbuilding shops, and fish weirs. Today only one private residence remains. Please respect their privacy.

2. Cadillac Mountain

At 1530 feet, Cadillac Mountain is the highest point within 50 miles of the coast from Maine to Rio de Janeiro in Brazil. Although Cadillac's summit is not the first place in the United States touched by the sun's rays each morning, visitors there may be the first people to see the sun dawn over America on a new day. Watching the sunrise and the sunset is a popular activity on the mountain.

While access by motor road is possible now, years ago the only way up Cadillac was by foot. For a time, the Green Mountain Railway Company operated a steam-driven cog railway line up the mountain's west side. Passengers took a buggy ride from Bar Harbor to a steam launch docked at the north end of Eagle Lake. The boat brought them to the railway terminus on the east shore of the lake. The trip by cog railway was so slow that passengers actually had time to jump off and pick blueberries along the way!

After seven years, the line went bust and the tracks were removed. The locomotive and cars still see service on the cog railway line up Mount Washington in New Hampshire.

Over the years, several hotels were built and were either torn or burned down. Today, the park service has rest rooms and a concession shop on the summit. There is no potable water.

While a trip to the top of the park's highest mountain is high on many hikers' lists, some find it anticlimactic after a long, hard climb to encounter the throngs of tourists, buses, and campers that crowd the summit on a typical day in season. Still, the walk is worth every effort.

There are few places where such stunning views unfold for 360 degrees. To the south lies the unbroken expanse of the Atlantic. Look closely and you'll swear you can see the curvature of the earth! That small smudge to the south with the flashing light is Mount Desert Rock, more than 25 miles offshore. Now automated, it is often used as a research station by scientists studying whales.

To the east, the Down East coast continues to Canada. In the west, the lesser peaks of Mount Desert Island lie in a row. In the distance look for Blue Hill and the Camden Hills.

MAP 2: CADILLAC MOUNTAIN

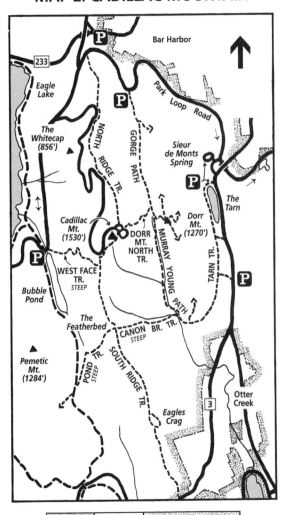

233

Bar Harbor

Eagle Lake

The Whitecap (856')

NORTH RIDGE TR.

GORGE PATH

Park Loop Road

Sieur de Monts Spring

The Tarn

Cadillac Mt. (1530')

DORR MT. NORTH TR.

Dorr Mt. (1270')

MURRAY YOUNG PATH

TARN TR.

WEST FACE TR. STEEP

Bubble Pond

The Featherbed

CANON BR. TR. STEEP

POND TR. STEEP

SOUTH RIDGE TR.

Pemetic Mt. (1284')

Eagles Crag

3

Otter Creek

0   ½   1   MILES   2

To the north lie the hills of Lucerne in Maine, nearly 40 miles off. When the sun is low in the morning, look closely at the horizon where those hills dip down. The gray silhouette behind is none other than mile-high Katahdin, the highest peak in Maine and the northern terminus of the Appalachian Trail. As the crow flies, Katahdin lies 150 miles away. That's excellent visibility in anyone's book.

TIP: While there is a well-developed site near the parking area that people believe is the summit, the high point of Cadillac Mountain is actually out behind the gift shop, where the radio antenna is located. To visit the true summit, follow the gravel road to the spot and look for the 3-inch U.S. Geological Survey benchmark cemented to a ledge.

Because of the large number of possible routes involving Cadillac Mountain trails, each trail is described separately. Mix and match to suit individual taste.

North Ridge Trail   *(Strenuous)*

This hike begins on the Park Loop Road directly across from the first overlook east of the intersection where the Loop Road becomes one-way. The trail rises steadily toward the summit, at times skirting the motor road. After leaving the road for the last time, about 1.5 miles from the start, the trail passes near a carving in a ledge. Legend has it that this is a Maltese cross left by explorer Samuel de Champlain's crew in 1604. Only a thin iron post betrays its location today.

The trail alternates between sections of scrub pines and open ledges on the just under 2-mile-long trip.

South Ridge Trail   *(Strenuous)*

One of the longest trails on Mount Desert Island, the South Ridge Trail up Cadillac is also one of the most popular. A feeder trail connects it directly with the nearby Blackwoods Campground.

Most people start by parking along the shoulder of Route 3 just west of the entrance to the campground. The trail ascends gradually for 0.75 mile before rising sharply onto Eagle's Crag. A small loop trail heads to the right here, and the views to the east make it worth the effort.

If you take the left path, you soon begin the long walk along the mountain's backbone. Take note as you leave the mixed woods and enter the world of bare ledge and jack pines; the vegetation change marks the line where the Great Fire of 1947 was stopped.

The trail continues its gradual rise, cresting over open ledge before descending slightly to a depression pond called the Featherbed, at 1.75 miles. Occasionally beavers live here, but the pond often dries up and is stagnant. Trail crews have built rustic benches here, so it is a good rest stop.

At the Featherbed intersection, the Canon Brook Trail enters from the east and the Pond Trail arrives from the west.

Climbing sharply now, the trail continues north, leaving most major vegetation behind. Winds here usually blow strongly. At 2 miles, the West Face Trail enters from the left. You will really notice the elevation gain now. Views abound in every direction.

After skirting the auto road, the trail heads more northeastward before arriving at the summit after a total of 3.5 miles.

When planning a loop trip, the South Ridge Trail is the best for descent, as it is easy on the knees and the best views are in front of you that way.

West Face Trail   *(Strenuous)*

A hike up the West Face Trail is one of the quickest ways to gain altitude on Cadillac. It is a very steep trail, however, and has several sections of smooth, steeply sloped granite ledges that make for tricky footing. It is a difficult trail to descend.

Begin at the Bubble Pond parking area on the Park Loop Road and walk to the north end of the lake. The trail begins shortly after you cross the outlet stream on a small bridge. Almost immediately the trail begins zigzagging up a series of steep ledges adorned with cedar and pine. There are excellent places to stop and enjoy views to the west and of the pond below.

After several steep pitches, the terrain opens up and the trail joins the South Ridge Trail at 0.85 mile.

Pond Trail   *(Strenuous)*

From the Featherbed, the Pond Trail heads west, skirting the north end of the wet ground and traversing smooth ledges in deep woods, and then drops like a rock off the west side of the mountain. Recent improvements by trail crews have added stone steps and some handrails to sections of loose dirt and rock that previously could be traversed only in a style that could be politely termed "a controlled crash."

New bog walk planks, footbridges, and stonework complete this renovation. The trail levels off after 0.25 mile and bottoms out in the marshy area between Cadillac and Pemetic before heading southwest to join with a carriage road at 1.5 miles.

Canon Brook Trail   *(Strenuous)*

The name Canon Brook is a classic mapmaker's mistake. Though it was originally Canyon Brook, a letter was dropped in later maps. Canyon makes more sense as a name, since the trail follows a steep, rocky streambed chasm.

From the Featherbed the trail hop, skips, and jumps on rocks down a muddy streambed heading east. After just over 0.5 mile, the trail turns hard right and begins following Canon Brook in earnest. Shortly the trail emerges onto ledges swept clean by spring torrents. Footing is tricky on the steep, smooth rock, and trail markers are sometimes hard to follow. Good boots are essential.

At 0.65 mile, the trail overlooks the actual canyon, which is about 10-feet wide and 15 feet deep. Continue carefully down the right side of the chasm to the boulders that offer steps down the overgrown talus slopes. The trail joins up with the Murray Young Path at a distance of 0.8 mile.

Murray Young Path   *(Strenuous)*

Reached from Route 3 via the Tarn Trail, the Murray Young Path offers one of the most interesting ways up Cadillac. Just after passing the Canon Brook Trail at 0.75 mile, this trail begins working its way up the brook that drains the valley between Cadillac and Dorr. Soon you pass a massive boulder in midstream with a memorial plaque to Young placed there by the Bar Harbor Village Improvement Association.

Past the boulder, the trail begins ascending more steeply, in places clinging to the west side of the gorge. One-half mile after the Canon Brook intersection, the trail enters a broad valley that once held a beaver pond. The trail has been relocated to the west here to avoid the muddy backwaters. However, the new route puts hikers through almost a quarter mile of Poison Ivy Central. The trail is narrow, and you must watch for those dreaded triple leaves very carefully.

After a steep, bouldery section at the head of the valley, the trail levels off over rocky ground and joins the cutoff trail between Cadillac and Dorr. Turn left and climb steeply for the last 0.5 mile to the Cadillac summit.

The Gorge Path   *(Strenuous)*

The 1.5-mile Gorge Path is one of the fastest—and in summer, coolest—ways to climb Cadillac. Begin on the Park Loop Road at the pull-off adjacent to the bridge spanning Kebo Brook, between Kebo Mountain and Cadillac.

The trail drops immediately to the cool, tree-lined shade beneath the bridge. It then follows the brook uphill before intersecting the Hemlock Trail in 0.5 mile. Shortly, the path gets much steeper as it crisscrosses the brook over large, mossy boulders. Even in high summer there is likely to be some water in pools and clefts along this route. There are no views to speak of; the real beauty of this path is in the forest details and weathered rocks.

After just under a mile, total, of steady climbing, the trail emerges from the dark forest into the cleft between Cadillac and Dorr Mountains. Turn right for another 0.5 mile of steep climbing over open ledges to the summit.

3. Dorr and Kebo Mountains

Dorr Mountain   (Strenuous)

There is only one way to describe the trails on Dorr Mountain—
straight up! Whether it is the Ladder Trail (with, according to trail
historian Tom St. Germain, exactly 1005 stone steps) or the Dorr
Mountain and East Face Trails, there is little respite until you are well
on your way to the top of this 1270-foot eminence.

At one time the Ladder Trail was the main access, and it is a
good place to start. Park on Route 3 near the wooden trailhead post
just south of the Tarn. A short downhill stretch brings you to an intersection with the Tarn Trail. Signs will point you to the base of the
Ladder Trail.

Almost immediately, steep stone steps ascend the side of the
mountain along an angled fault in the granite. The rise is steady, almost unforgiving, for 0.5 mile, but the views come quickly. There
are no sources of water, and in summer the sun mercilessly bakes
the rock faces.

Just as the trail levels out, it meets with the Dorr Mountain Trail.
Bear left for the meandering yet steady trip to the relatively small and
rock-strewn summit, for a total hike of just under a mile.

Views include the activity on Cadillac Mountain to the west and
nice angles on Bar Harbor and Frenchman Bay to the north and the
ocean to the south.

Return by retracing your steps down the Dorr Mountain Trail. To
take it, turn left and head north. Both this trail and the closely routed
East Face Trail will bring you down near the south end of the Tarn.
The Tarn Trail back along the west side of the lake traverses large
boulders and in places bears little resemblance to a trail.

Another option is to take the more gradual South Ridge Trail
down 1.2 miles, and turn left on the comparatively flat Canon
Brook/Tarn Trail for a longer loop of 3 miles.

MAP 3: DORR & KEBO MTNS.

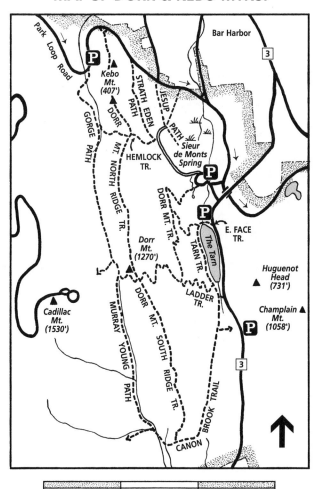

Park Loop Road

Bar Harbor

3

P

Kebo
Mt.
(407')

STRATH EDEN PATH

JESUP PATH

GORGE PATH

DORR MT. NORTH RIDGE TR.

HEMLOCK TR.

Sieur
de Monts
Spring

P

DORR MT. TR.

TARN TR.

P

E. FACE
TR.

The Tarn

Dorr
Mt.
(1270')

Huguenot
Head
(731')

LADDER
TR.

Cadillac
Mt.
(1530')

MURRAY YOUNG PATH

DORR MT. SOUTH RIDGE TR.

Champlain ▲
Mt.
(1058')

P

3

BROOK TRAIL

CANON

0   ½   1   MILES   1½

Kebo Mountain   (Moderate)

With three small summits and numerous vegetation zones, Kebo Mountain is a great short hike.

Begin on the Park Loop Road at a dirt turnoff several hundred yards past the trailhead post at the north end of the mountain. Trail crews have recently erected a trail sign and restored the Strath Eden Path, which begins at this parking spot, although most maps have yet to catch up and include it. The path is fairly level as it heads south along the mountain's eastern flank. Several old roads branch off to the right and end shortly at small abandoned quarry sites. The trail rises gradually and then drops steadily to where it meets the Hemlock Trail between Kebo and Dorr Mountains. Turn right here and begin the steady ascent. Some stretches are steep.

At the next intersection between the two mountains, turn right again and climb the first of Kebo's knobs. The trail drops steeply and heads north, gradually climbing the second hump. Open ledges along the way provide wonderful views of Cadillac to the west and Great Meadow Marsh and Bar Harbor to the east. Just north of the marsh a bottling plant, now long gone, once packaged Kebo Valley spring water for sale around the country.

Descend again and pass through interesting groves of varying forest types. Watch out for a sharp left turn. Ascend the final peak through a grove of jack pines growing from barren granite ledges. The summit, at 407 feet, is just ahead.

Below you can see portions of the Kebo Valley Golf Course, the ninth oldest in North America.

Continue north and descend steeply. Just before reaching the loop road you come to a very slippery and steep section that will require the use of hands. Turn right after hitting the road for the short jaunt back to the start, for a total distance of just over 1.5 miles.

4. Champlain Mountain Area

Champlain Mountain

One of the most popular mountains in the park, 1058-foot Champlain Mountain is home to one of the most rugged and dangerous trails on the East Coast: The Precipice.

There are several ways up—and perhaps more important, down—Champlain. Its wide-open summit has spectacular views in all directions. It is the best place to sit and watch all the comings and goings in Frenchman Bay to the east. Whale-watch, lobster, excursion, and pleasure boats race to and fro among the Porcupine Islands, named years ago for their distinctive shapes.

Each morning the *Bluenose* international ferry leaves Bar Harbor for Yarmouth, Nova Scotia, carrying up to 1,000 passengers and hundreds of cars and trucks. The red flashing light of the Egg Rock Lighthouse, now automated, will help guide it on its return later the same night.

The Precipice Trail   *(Ladder)*

A sign at the trailhead in the parking lot on the Park Loop Road warns that The Precipice is not so much a hiking trail as a non-technical climbing route. This cannot be overstated.

Although fatalities are rare on this trail and are usually confined to those who wander off the trail or have an accident while doing technical climbing, scores of people each year misjudge their abilities and need assistance to get down.

WARNING: Do not attempt this trail if you have a fear of heights, are not properly dressed, lack proper footwear, or are not physically prepared. Do not leave late in the day when there will not be adequate daylight to complete your hike. Also, this trail has no water, ever. Hikers can be exposed to the sun, wind, or rain for extended periods. Even relatively level sections can be slippery and hazardous after a rain.

MAP 4: CHAMPLAIN MTN. AREA

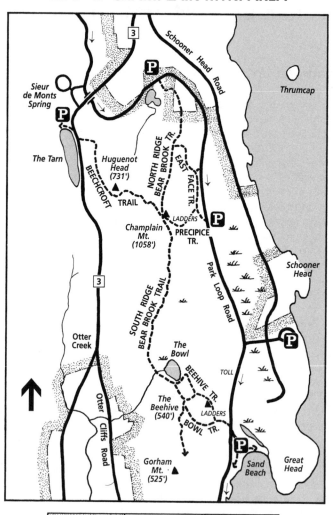

Schooner Head Road

3

P

Thrumcap

Sieur de Monts Spring

P

The Tarn

Huguenot Head (731')

NORTH RIDGE BEAR BROOK TR.

BEECHCROFT TRAIL

EAST FACE TR.

LADDERS

Champlain Mt. (1058')

PRECIPICE TR.

P

3

Schooner Head

Park Loop Road

Otter Creek

SOUTH RIDGE BEAR BROOK TRAIL

The Bowl

BEEHIVE TR.

TOLL

The Beehive (540')

LADDERS

BOWL TR.

Otter Cliffs Road

P

Gorham Mt. (525')

Sand Beach

Great Head

P

0   ½   1   1½

MILES

Begin on the steps that lead west from the parking area on the Park Loop Road. The trail runs over ledge and boulders for a few hundred yards to the first ladder rung and handrail at the base of a cliff. The "step up" here is 5 feet. Rangers like to call this spot "The Eliminator," since people who have trouble here usually have enough good sense to turn back.

After the first rung, the trail rises sharply as it heads north to the base of a large boulder field. Climb steeply here, often using your hands, as you follow trail markers over and under truck-sized rocks. The cliffs overlooking the boulder field are often home to endangered peregrine falcons, which were reintroduced to the park some years back. Each year a pair returns to raise their chicks on a lofty ledge called a scrape. Until the birds are fledged the Precipice Trail is closed, to make sure human activity doesn't hurt nesting efforts. Those who fail to heed closed area signs can be summonsed.

Leaving the boulder field behind, the trail continues up, passing over a wooden footbridge with the aid of extensive iron handrails. Switchbacks continue north, then south, as more altitude is gained.

The trail turns sharply to the left where the East Face Trail enters from the right. Hands are needed to boost yourself up 5- and 6-foot-high steps as the trail continues.

Watch to avoid false trails at major turns. So many people make the same mistakes that the stray paths can look like the main trail. If you encounter a dead end or piles of sticks or rocks in the path, turn back.

The upper third of The Precipice consists of several switchbacks connected by a series of iron bars pounded into the cliff face as ladder rungs. Several iron ladders are also attached as climbing aids.

In some areas, iron bars act as guardrails to catch feet that may slip on narrow ledges. Some handrails are provided. Since dropoffs of several hundred feet are common, watch your step carefully. Try to keep three points of contact with the rock (i.e., two hands and one foot, or two feet and one hand) at all times.

Just as the trail seems to curve to the left and disappear at the top of a huge drop, you enter a cleft and are back on solid ground. The trail continues, steeply at times, up the open jack pine woods and over ledges to the summit, for a total trip of just over a mile.

Rather than return via The Precipice, which is more difficult than climbing up and can cause climber jams on busy days, consider taking the North Ridge Trail down.

The Beechcroft Trail, which traverses Huguenot Head on its way to the summit of Champlain, branches off the North Ridge Trail just a little north of the summit. It is very steep and treacherous in spots.

North Ridge Trail   *(Strenuous)*

From the summit, the North Ridge, or Bear Brook, Trail heads north over open ledges and through small groves of stunted trees. Watch carefully near the top, since idiots insist on building scores of small cairns, which can make staying on the right trail difficult.

Along the entire way there will be great views of Bar Harbor and the renowned genetic research facility of Jackson Laboratory to the north.

About halfway down, keep your eyes out for a circular bronze survey marker with the initials "JDR." It is one of the original benchmarks used by crews working for John D. Rockefeller Jr. as he helped to assemble land to create Acadia National Park.

About 0.5 mile from the summit, turn right onto the East Face Trail. Descend steeply to a curved path paved with flat granite boulders. A right turn will connect you, over a difficult trail, to the lower Precipice. A left will take you to the Park Loop Road over smooth ledges. A right here leaves you only a 0.5-mile walk back to your vehicle along the Park Loop Road. Total distance for the circuit is 2.25 miles.

Staying on the North Ridge/Bear Brook Trail brings you quickly to the parking area on the Loop Road at the north end of the mountain. This is a good route to climb and return if the weather is questionable.

South Ridge Trail   *(Strenuous)*

The South Ridge section of the Bear Brook Trail leaves the summit and gradually descends toward the Beehive and the Bowl. This route offers fine views of the ocean and areas to the east and west. Crossing the Bowl outlet stream on a small bridge, the trail skirts this high mountain pond. Turn right on the Bowl trail for the quick descent to the Loop Road near Sand Beach. Take a left on the Loop Road, and it is a 1.5-mile walk back to your car.

Huguenot Head   *(Moderate)*

Built by craftsmen nearly 100 years ago, the Beechcroft Trail up Huguenot Head is one of the most handsome on the island. Its 1,500 winding stone steps and easy grades are so reminiscent of a Hobbit road that one almost expects to see Bilbo Baggins strutting down the trail at every turn.

Park in the paved area on the west side of Route 3, just south of the park's Sieur de Monts entrance. The trail starts at the wooden marker and stone steps directly across the road. Maintaining a gradual incline, the path works up the western side of a small hill and then crosses over onto the steep side of Huguenot Head itself. Here numerous switchbacks help hikers gain altitude quickly. Especially in summer, the sun bakes these ledges, and there is no water, so be sure to carry some.

After about 0.5 mile, the trail skirts the actual summit, which can be reached by a quick and easy bushwhack, and drops down into a small seasonal pond before rising steeply to the summit of Champlain Mountain. Deer tracks are often seen in the mud around the pond.

Just before you descend toward the pond, you'll cross fine open ledges that offer splendid views of the ocean to the south and Dorr and Cadillac Mountains to the west. Below lies the Tarn, a small, shallow pond formed by a dam built by George B. Dorr, one of the fathers of the park and its first superintendent.

The Beehive   *(Ladder)*

For a short hike that is long on challenge and reward, yet short on distance and elevation gain, the aptly named, 540-foot-tall Beehive is a good choice.

The trail begins just north of the entrance to the Sand Beach parking area and rises gradually over recently rebuilt stepping-stones. After a short distance the incline increases and several sloping, yet open ledges are crossed. The ladder trail goes right at the first intersection, just under 0.25 mile from the start. It quickly begins a series of switchbacks up the carved face of the Beehive. Views of Sand Beach, Great Head, and the entire Ocean Drive start immediately and just keep getting better.

In several places, narrow footbridges have been installed, including a unique one composed of iron bars set horizontally. Hands are definitely needed, and foot- and handrails are occasionally provided.

One last steep section is passed before reaching the top at 0.5 mile.

To return, continue north on the Beehive Trail. You can take a shortcut by turning left at the first intersection and descending steeply over boulder fields. A left at the next intersection will take you back toward Sand Beach. Or, continue on to The Bowl, a high, nearly round pond hidden behind the Beehive. Stop for a minute to soak your tired feet before skirting the south end of the pond to the next trail intersection. Turn left there, climb briefly, and then descend steadily back toward Sand Beach, for a total walk of just under 1.5 miles.

5. Great Head and Gorham Mountain

Great Head   (Easy)

This short, moderately easy hike provides excellent views of the island's rocky coast and out to the horizon on the stormy Atlantic.

Although the 2-mile loop can be done by fording the small stream on the east end of Sand Beach, the best place to start is at the paved parking area on the dead-end park road that heads south from the Schooner Head Overlook intersection.

Hit the trail and take your first obvious left. The path, which is quite wide although rocky, descends gradually toward the shore. Numerous bootleg trails cut down to the massive granite ledges with their fine views and numerous tide pools.

Stay to the left as you continue through an intersection and up to the high point of 145-foot Great Head. The rubble of a stone tower, once used as a tea house, is evident at the top.

Continue west along the peninsula. Fabulous views of Ocean Drive, Newport Cove, and the ledge called "Old Soaker" will unfold. Do not try to descend to the many ocean caves along the cliff face; several people, including well-trained and well-equipped technical climbers, have died in the attempt.

The most unusual geologic feature on this walk is Sand Beach. More than just sand, much of the beach is made up of crushed bits of shells. In summer, swimmers brave the brisk 54-degree waters.

In 1911 the schooner *Tay,* with a cargo of lumber, ran aground on Sand Beach, scattering its load. The ribs of the vessel sometimes still protrude when waves carve the dunes at the back of the beach.

Head north on the trail, which now traverses the remains of an old road, to return to the parking area, or take a right at the trail intersection just south of the Sand Beach turnoff, to cut back east across the head through a grove of young white birch. All the vegetation on Great Head is still recovering from the effects of the Great

MAP 5: GREAT HEAD & GORHAM MTN.

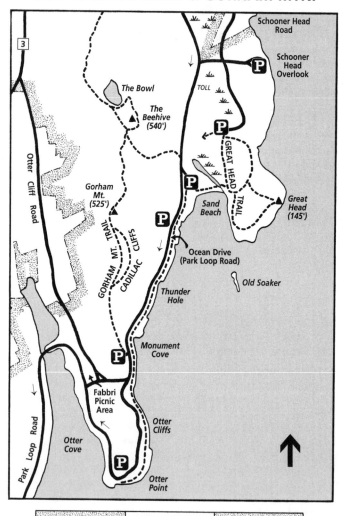

Schooner Head Road

Schooner Head Overlook

The Bowl

The Beehive (540')

TOLL

GREAT HEAD TRAIL

Gorham Mt. (525')

Sand Beach

Great Head (145')

GORHAM MT. TRAIL

CADILLAC CLIFFS

Otter Cliff Road

Ocean Drive (Park Loop Road)

Old Soaker

Thunder Hole

Monument Cove

Fabbri Picnic Area

Otter Cliffs

Park Loop Road

Otter Cove

Otter Point

3

0   ½   1   1½

MILES

Fire of '47, which blew itself out in a great, wind-whipped fireball that leapt from the head and extinguished itself out over the ocean.

Gorham Mountain   (Moderate)

A hike up 525-foot Gorham Mountain along the Ocean Drive in Acadia National Park traverses some of the most interesting and diverse terrain the island has to offer.

The walk begins at the Gorham Mountain parking area on the right about 0.25 mile from Thunder Hole. The trail leaves the northwest corner of the lot, passing over uneven ledge as it begins a gradual ascent. In spring and after heavy rains this trail can be very wet.

About 0.4 mile from the start is an intersection. On the south face of a massive boulder here is a bronze plaque dedicated to "Waldron Bates, Pathfinder." Bates, a Philadelphia lawyer, was instrumental in the layout and design of numerous trails on the island's eastern side.

Although the trail splits here, it will rejoin later on. Take the Cadillac Cliffs Trail to the right and descend slightly before traversing the base of the cliffs that make up the mountain's southern flank. This path has you going over and even under massive boulders. In several places it is easy to see, from the way in which the rocks are worn, that the cliffs were once the shoreline when sea levels were higher. After about 0.5 mile, the trail rejoins the main path, which sticks to the ridge line.

Several more steep ascents are needed before breaking out onto the wide, open summit at just under a mile from the start. Views are spectacular, from Sand Beach to the east to Otter Cliffs to the west. To the north, Cadillac, Dorr, and Champlain Mountains loom. Leave extra time to tarry at the summit.

Return using the ridgeline trail to the parking lot. *Or* continue north, dropping steeply at times, into the valley between Gorham and Halfway Mountains. Turn right on the Bowl Trail, which will take you back to the Ocean Drive. Head right again and take the shore walk, which parallels the Ocean Drive, back to the parking area, for a total hike of 2.5 miles (slightly less via the ridgeline trail).

6. Day Mountain and Hunter's Beach

Day Mountain   (Moderate)

Day Mountain is another of Acadia's lesser peaks that offers rewards far beyond its 583-foot summit height.

The trail starts in Seal Harbor across from the parking area on Route 3, about 1.5 miles west of Blackwoods Campground. Just down the road is a monument to Samuel de Champlain, who named Mount Desert Island in 1604. The land around the monument was the first nucleus of what eventually became Acadia National Park. The trail rises gently through open woods and crosses a carriage road a little over 0.25 mile from its start.

The way becomes more steep, but remains moderate, for another 0.25 mile before again crossing a carriage road. Here walkers have a choice. They can continue on the trail to the summit, crossing the meandering summit carriage road once more, or they can take the carriage road the rest of the way. I like the carriage road route myself, as it offers better views in more directions.

For more adventurous types, a visit to the Day Mountain caves is in order. At the second carriage road crossing, go right for 100 yards or so then bushwhack north along the base of the cliffs. About 0.25 mile along are the caves. A trail once led up through one of them on a wooden ladder to the carriage road above. A dead-end cave on the right is big enough for several people to squeeze into, provided they are not claustrophobic! At last report the ladders were rotted and had not been replaced, so do not attempt to climb them.

From the summit, where guided carriage rides from the nearby Wildwood Stable pause to savor the sunset, views extend 360 degrees. A foot trail to the north leads down to the stable complex.

Retrace your steps, or vary the route by using the carriage road to return to your car, for a total trip of about 2 miles.

MAP 6: DAY MTN. & HUNTER'S BEACH

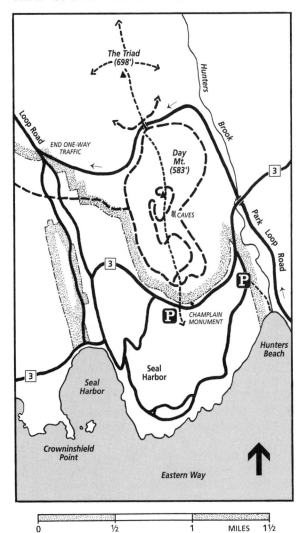

Hunter's Beach   (Easy)

Hunter's Beach is one of the quintessential spots on Mount Desert Island that typify the natural beauty and splendor of this place. To reach the parking area, head west on Route 3 and take the first left about 0.8 mile past the entrance to the Blackwoods Campground. The trailhead is about 0.2 mile farther on the left.

There is only enough room for five or six cars here, and that is as it should be; if Hunter's Beach becomes overrun, no one will be able to enjoy its magic. If the lot is full, please consider coming back later or trying another day.

The trail begins on level ground behind the parking area and then quickly begins its descent toward the cobble beach about a half mile away. After a short distance, an elaborate footbridge, built by volunteer trail crews, is crossed. The trail then drops more over a complicated pattern of tree roots. On the left, Hunter's Brook can first be heard, then seen. The trail follows the brook a short ways, crossing a side channel on boulders. Listen now for the roar of the waves, and notice whether you can smell the salt spray. The final 200-foot section of trail passes through thick trees, which frame a magnificent view of the offshore waters that unfolds as you emerge from the forest.

Hunter's Beach itself is a typical steep cobble beach composed of stones rounded and worn smooth by the sea. It is barely 100 yards long and wedged between high cliffs. The stone slope is re-formed with each storm. When the waves are large enough you can hear the stones tumbling over each other as the currents churn them over and over. Crushed lobster traps and worn driftwood above the seaweed line marking high tide testify to the ocean's power. Often, Hunter's Brook disappears into the rocks only to emerge lower on the shore.

At low tide, be sure to explore the steep chasm to the east. Notice how the ocean exploits the weakness of the rock, eroding the schist faster than the stronger granite. Smooth ledges here make a great picnic spot.

7. Pemetic Mountain

Pemetic Mountain Loop   *(Strenuous)*

Despite its major status, with a summit of 1248 feet, Pemetic Mountain does not experience the same heavy use as other island mountains.

Only one loop hike is possible without more than a mile of hoofing it on a busy paved road. The most popular route up Pemetic begins at the Bubble Pond parking area along the Park Loop Road. Here park officials actually tore up a paved parking lot on the lakeshore and replaced it with a paradise in the form of new trees and shrubs.

Take the carriage road south. The trail heads off to the right in 0.1 mile. Starting gradually, the Pemetic Trail gets steadily steeper as it climbs through open spruce woods. After 0.5 mile it levels off some, and the first views to the east open up as the path follows the top of steep cliffs. After the trail turns away from the east slope, the incline moderates. The Bubbles–Pemetic Trail enters from the right at 0.9 mile. The top is reached after a total walk of 1.25 miles. The summit consists of several independent granite knobs, and there are good views in all directions.

To make a long loop, head south down the West Cliff Trail from the summit. You will pass several interesting small marshes nestled in bowls carved out of the mountain's granite. At the intersection in 0.5 mile, the trail to the left offers a shortcut, but is extremely steep and wet in places. Continue straight for another 0.5 mile to the Pond Trail between Pemetic and some high ground to the south called the Triad. Turn left and descend gradually on a relatively smooth path for 0.6 mile to a carriage road. Left on the carriage road will take you back 1.5 miles to the start, for a total distance of just under 4.5 miles.

Bubbles–Pemetic Trail   *(Strenuous)*

Another possible up-and-back route to Pemetic's summit is the Bubbles Pemetic Trail. It rises steeply from the Bubbles parking lot

MAP 7: PEMETIC MOUNTAIN

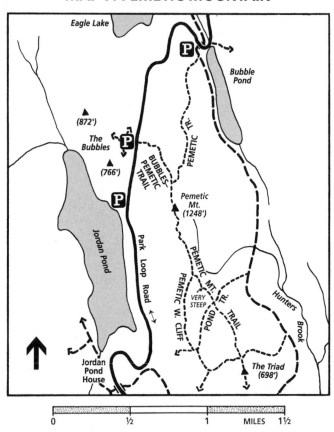

(Bubbles–Pemetic Trail, continued)

on the Park Loop Road. About halfway up, the trail enters a narrow
canyon and streambed more than 15 feet deep. A wooden ladder
at the end allows hikers to escape. Those who prefer to avoid the
ladder can use a bypass trail on the south side of the chasm.

8. West of Jordan Pond

Sargent Mountain   *(Strenuous)*

The furthest removed from any paved roads, and with foot access only, the 1373-foot summit of Sargent Mountain is the wildest and most alpine of any in the park. Its broad, open, windswept plain, shrubby vegetation, and lichen-encrusted rock make this peak similar to those above treeline in the White Mountains or Baxter State Park.

The best walk up Sargent Mountain begins at the Parkman Mountain parking area on the east side of Route 198, where it crests on its way into Northeast Harbor. Follow the carriage road out of the parking area and turn right, then left after a short distance. Stay on the winding carriage road for just under a mile. Stop at the second of two graceful granite arch bridges and turn left on the Hadlock Brook Trail.

In spring, or after a moderate rainfall, the waterfall on Hadlock Brook, the tallest on Mount Desert Island, should be in full force as clear waters splash down the 30-foot drop.

From here, the trail crisscrosses the brook on a moderate grade. After crossing the brook for the last time, the trail begins to climb very steeply until it reaches some open granite ledges, which provide good views to the west. A short section of trail through shrubby trees, then one last steep incline over bare rock, and you are on the open ridgeline. Turn left for the just over 0.5-mile stroll to the summit over vast blueberry barrens and bare rock. In late summer, striking red-orange wood lilies, which are found in only a very few exposed mountain and coastal locations, are in bloom.

Tufted grass and dark, mysterious rain pools give Sargent an almost tundra-like feel. Heavy winds from any direction are not uncommon. Total distance to the top is approximately 2 miles.

At one time a wooden fire tower was located at the summit, but only a massive cairn of weathered rock remains. Rusting wire

MAP 8: WEST OF JORDAN POND

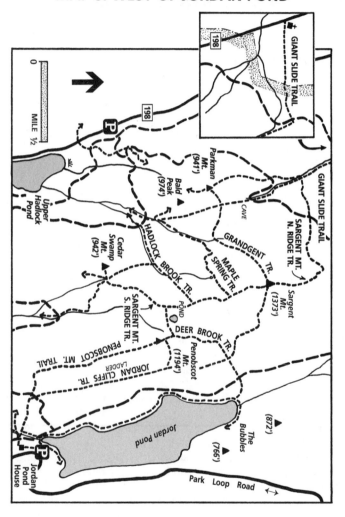

and an occasional iron bar in the ledge are the only evidence of past structures.

To return, backtrack to the last major intersection and turn right toward Maple Spring. Located at a low spot on the mountainside, this spring has water most of the year. The trail rises for a short distance over one of Sargent's arms before dropping steeply through thick forest in a series of switchbacks.

After 0.5 mile it turns sharply south and descends into the valley created by one branch of Hadlock Brook. The trail follows the tumbling and cascading brook back to the first carriage road bridge you crossed. Turn west here and return to the car by the carriage road. Total trip distance is about 4 miles.

Giant Slide Trail   *(Strenuous)*

Another route up Sargent begins along Route 198 near an old stone church. Park along the shoulder and follow the private dirt road/driveway east for 0.4 mile. The Giant Slide Trail takes off where the road turns sharply left. Ascend slowly through forest decorated with large boulders.

After crossing a carriage road, the trail turns sharply right and begins ascending steeply to the south. It follows a brook that sports beautiful small falls and water tumbling over boulders. In the clefts in the rock the sun never shines. It is not unusual to find ice and snow patches here in late May.

About 0.5 mile from the carriage road is an intersection. A trail on the left rises steeply over another carriage road and up the north side of Sargent to the summit in about 2.1 miles. A right turn takes you up steeply through some pretty woods and over another carriage road to the summit of Parkman Mountain.

Stay straight, and the trail soon levels off and crosses a carriage road. Just ahead is a "cave" created when a massive slab of granite calved off a nearby cliff and slid into the brook. The trail goes through the 25-foot-long cave on stepping-stones in the water. During high water it may be impassable.

Soon another intersection is reached. Left heads up the Grandgent Trail to the summit of Sargent, for a total walk of 2.25 miles. Right rises steeply to the top of Parkman. Straight brings you through a narrow valley where a central spring creates streams that flow in two directions, north and south. The trail continues a steady descent, often on loose rocks, to the carriage road on the other side of Bald Peak.

Penobscot Mountain   *(Strenuous)*

Penobscot Mountain also offers fine views and a wide, barren ridge and summit. At 1194 feet, it is the fifth highest on the island.

Begin in the Jordan Pond House overflow parking area, located at the south end of the pond just off the Park Loop Road. Take the path to the Pond House itself and past the gift shop to the trail that leads west down a short hill to the carriage road. The trail begins on a footbridge just across the carriage road and slightly to the right.

The path begins to rise immediately, with several steeper sections. A set of stone steps leads to the next carriage road crossing in 0.5 mile. The Penobscot Mountain Trail begins straight across on steep ledges that may require the use of hands.

The trail zigzags up the east side of the mountain, occasionally using wooden handrails and plank bridges. At one point the trail, about 5 feet wide, has a smooth cliff 20 feet high on the left and a drop of 30 to 40 feet on the right. Rough footing can lead to ankle injuries here, and in several spots, hikers must use their hands to help boost themselves up narrow clefts.

After about another 0.25 mile the trail levels out. Where it emerges from the woods there are smooth ledges and wonderful views to the east.

After a short distance the trail turns sharply right and begins the ascent over open barren ledge. Several major plateaus, which turn out to be false summits, are encountered. Finally, in just over 1.5 mile, the summit is reached. Again, there are great views in all directions.

From the summit, head north down a steep and sometimes slippery incline to the col between Sargent and Penobscot. Stay straight at the intersection and walk the easy 0.1 mile to Sargent Mountain Pond, a cool, welcome respite on hot days. Once called Lake of the

Clouds, and also known locally as the Frog Pond, Sargent Mountain Pond is a great place for a quick dip or to stop for lunch. Trail crews have built several log benches at this site.

After a swim, head back to the col intersection and turn left to head down the Deer Brook Trail. Descend quickly and pass un-marked Cedar Spring. About 0.5 mile from the col intersection another intersection is reached.

Jordan Cliffs Trail   *(Ladder)*

At this next intersection, the trail to the left ascends the east side of Sargent, and the one to the right is the Jordan Cliffs Trail. This will return you along the mountain's east face. It is very precip-itous and there are several places where ladder rungs and hand rail-ings are needed.

Alternatively, continue straight at the intersection and descend along the brook. Just before coming out on a carriage road, you must negotiate a massive tangle of tree roots. These roots beneath you feet are film stars, however. They were featured in a scene in the Stephen King horror movie *Pet Sematary*.

Once at the carriage road, stroll to the left to check out another unique granite bridge. Then head south on the carriage road back toward the Jordan Pond House, for a hike of just under 4 miles.

Another option is to take the trail at the bridge that descends to the shore of Jordan Pond. Turn right and follow the Jordan Pond Trail along the water's edge back to the starting point.

9. Around Jordan Pond

(Easy)

At just over 3 miles, the walk around Jordan Pond can't be called short, although since it sports few changes in elevation it is considered an easy walk. The pond is a reservoir, and swimming and wading are not allowed. Aside from the occasional log footbridge or assemblage of stepping-stones, the path, which skirts the lake for its entire journey, is not especially difficult to negotiate.

Because the Jordan Pond House restaurant and gift shop is often crowded, begin your walk in the boat ramp parking area located at the south end of the pond, just off the Park Loop Road. Walk to the bottom of the boat ramp road and turn right. Be sure to pause here for one of the most impressive vistas in the park. At the north end of the pond are the Bubbles, reportedly an adaptation of the term "bubbies." Legend also holds they were named by a summer gentleman who said the distinctive mounds reminded him of his rather well-endowed girlfriend named Bubbles. Either way, the path runs smoothly for 0.25 mile, and crosses a marshy cove on a causeway of large flat stones. A side trail here turns east and connects with the Park Loop Road.

The trail heads north for nearly a mile to an intersection with the trail from the Bubbles parking area. This is another possible starting and ending point for the loop.

As the trail skirts the base of South Bubble, check the cliffs above for technical climbers. The trail here involves a lot of hopping from large boulder to large boulder, but crews from the Youth Conservation Corps have done a great job in recent years hauling soil to smooth the way. At the north end of the pond, the trail passes an intersection with the trail that ascends steeply between the Bubbles. It then crosses a stream on a unique A-frame truss bridge made of logs. After an intersection with a trail that heads north and west to connect with a carriage road higher up the mountain, the path heads back down the western side of the lake.

MAP 9: AROUND JORDAN POND

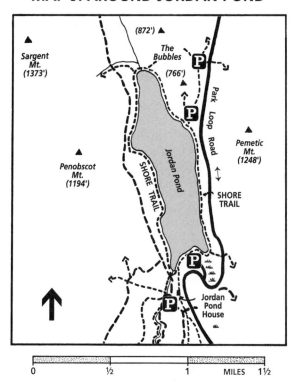

If you are tired of walking along the lake, take the trail to the carriage road. It rises very steeply and ends near a magnificent arched bridge. Both the trail and the carriage road will lead you back to the Jordan Pond House.

After crossing the Jordan Pond outlet stream, head east again to the launch ramp and your car.

If you time things right, stop at the Jordan Pond House for their famous tea and popovers on the lawn. It is an island tradition going back nearly 100 years. Hiking attire is just fine.

10. The Bubbles and Conners Nubble

North and South Bubbles   (Moderate)

South Bubble (766 feet) is one of the most popular climbs in the park, and only moderately strenuous. In recent years, trail crews have heavily rebuilt some sections to reduce erosion and make footing easier. The result is a heavily engineered trail that gets the job done but lacks the wilderness ambience preferred by some hikers.

The most direct route begins at the Bubbles parking area on the Park Loop Road. The trail leaves the west side of the lot and heads west. Turn right after 100 yards. Stay on this trail as it curves gradually to the west on an old logging road. After a short distance, the trail turns hard left and due west as it rises steeply on log and stone steps to the swale between the twin peaks. A right turn partway up at a major intersection will take you up a very steep and rugged trail to the top of the somewhat higher (872 feet) North Bubble.

Continue straight, however, to go to South Bubble, and in less than 0.5 mile from the start, go left at the next intersection over more gradual inclines for another 0.25 mile to the top.

Along the way take one of the easy-to-follow, yet unmarked side trails to visit Bubble Rock. The size of a small house, this boulder is a glacial erratic left atop the Bubble when an ice sheet a mile thick retreated more than 10,000 years ago.

Originally Mount Desert Island was one large ridge running in an east-west direction. As the glacier overtopped it from the north it finally cut through, leaving the north-south ridges seen today. Lakes filled the deep cuts between the hills. As the ice moved southward, it created smooth inclines on the north sides of hills as it rode up and over. On the southerly slopes, it tore off large blocks of rock, leaving the cliffs evident today. According to geologist Carleton Chapman, Bubble Rock was torn from another mountain more than 20 miles to the northwest.

MAP 10: THE BUBBLES & CONNERS NUBBLE

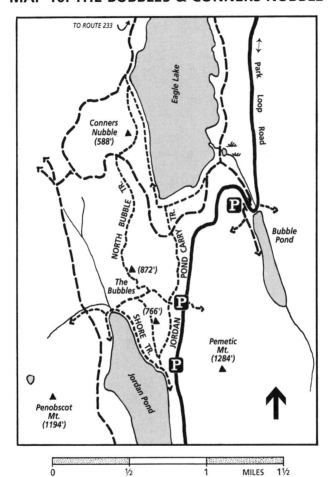

TO ROUTE 233

Eagle Lake

Park Loop Road

Conners
Nubble
(588')

Bubble
Pond

NORTH BUBBLE TR.

POND CARRY TR.

(872')

The
Bubbles

(766')

SHORE TR.

Pemetic
Mt.
(1284')

JORDAN

Jordan Pond

Penobscot
Mt.
(1194')

| 0 | ½ | 1 | MILES | 1½ |

Back on the trail, pass the summit at just over 0.5 mile from the start and continue down slightly to the ledges overlooking Jordan Pond to the south. The cliffs below are popular with technical climbers.

To vary your route back, turn left at the intersection in the swale and drop steeply over loose boulders to the north end of Jordan Pond. Go left again for 0.5 mile to the Jordan Pond Carry Trail intersection, then turn left once more for about 0.5 mile until it is time to turn right for the 100-yard-long path to the parking area.

Conners Nubble *(Moderate)*

Standing on the summit of Conners Nubble, overlooking Eagle Lake and dwarfed by massive mountains to the east and west, you cannot help but feel like the conductor of some antediluvian orchestra embraced by the instruments of earth's majesty.

Start by parking at the north end of Eagle Lake on Route 233 and heading south on the carriage road down the west side of the lake. About 1.5 miles from the start, take the trail that heads left and across a swampy area. Turn right at the first intersection. (A left turn leads around the shore of the lake on a very rough track.) The trail then begins a gradual ascent through open woods on the Nubble's north slope. Just before hitting the flat, open summit, at just under 2 miles from the start, the trail becomes steeper. Careful foot placement is necessary.

The open, steplike nature of the 588-foot summit provides endless nooks where you can escape from the constant wind. Eagle Lake shimmers below to the east, with Cadillac Mountain rising steeply behind. To the south, Pemetic Mountain and the North Bubble are almost close enough to touch. Sargent and Penobscot Mountains tower to the west.

Retrace your steps, or take the short, but sometimes very steep, trail that continues southwest to the carriage road around the lake. Turn right and stay right at the next road intersection to return to your vehicle. Total distance is just under 4 miles if you return by the same route, 5 miles if you take the alternative trail and carriage road.

11. Norumbega Mountain

(Strenuous)

When French explorer Samuel de Champlain first sighted Mount Desert Island in 1604, he was on a mission of discovery. His goal was the fabled golden-walled city of Norumbega, which native tribesmen said existed somewhere in the vicinity of present-day Bangor. Over the years Bangor grew to be "The Queen City" and hub of lumbering in Maine. For many who made their fortune there, it was indeed a city of gold.

Champlain was not the only one bitten by the legend, and naming the mountain that looms on the eastern side of Somes Sound Norumbega recognizes the legend's significance in local history.

Most hikes up Norumbega begin at the parking area above Upper Hadlock Pond along Route 198. The Goat Trail, aptly named due to its steep ascent, begins here and climbs quickly up the mountain's eastern flank. After 0.25 mile the trail takes a more gradual incline on the way to the 852-foot summit (0.5 mile from the start). In season, blueberries provide a refreshing trailside treat.

While views from the summit are grand, Norumbega is not broad and open like most of the island's larger peaks.

The trail continues south, passing through open coniferous forest, descending gradually toward the south end of Lower Hadlock Pond. This is a water supply; no swimming or wading allowed.

At the trail intersection, a right turn will take you a short way to the Northeast Harbor Golf Course. Straight leads to a parking spot near the dam. A left turn on the trail that runs along the west shore of the pond is worth the trip, and allows you to return to your start with only minimal elevation gain, for a total trip of about 2.5 miles.

MAP 11: NORUMBEGA MTN.

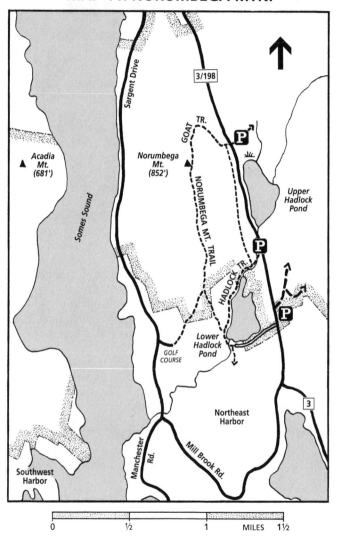

Sargent Drive

3/198

GOAT TR.

Acadia Mt. (681')

Norumbega Mt. (852')

NORUMBEGA MT. TRAIL

P

P

Upper Hadlock Pond

HADLOCK TR.

P

Somes Sound

Lower Hadlock Pond

GOLF COURSE

Northeast Harbor

3

Manchester Rd.

Mill Brook Rd.

Southwest Harbor

0   ½   1   MILES   1½

12. Parkman and Cedar Swamp Mountains

Parkman Mountain and Bald Peak   (Moderate)

Parkman Mountain, 941 feet in height, and its sister summit Bald Peak, at 974 feet, are often bypassed by those on the way to higher summits to the east. But that is their loss.

Begin at the Parkman Mountain parking area on the east side of Route 198 where it crests on the way into Northeast Harbor. Follow the carriage road out of the parking area and turn right, then left after a short distance. Stay on the winding carriage road for less than 0.25 mile until you see the Parkman Mountain trail post on the left. After turning here, you will ascend gradually, cross another carriage road after a few yards, and then plunge into the quiet forest. The trail zigzags up an unnamed ridge with occasional views. Some sections are steep with slick footing and may require the use of hands, although dropoffs are not great.

After 0.75 mile you enter the col between Parkman Mountain and Bald Peak. A left takes you quickly to the summit of Parkman, a right to Bald Peak on well-marked trails.

Parkman offers splendid views of sheltered Somesville to the northwest. The earliest permanent village on Mount Desert Island was founded here in 1761, originally called Betwixt the Hills.

Bald Peak has good views of Upper Hadlock Pond immediately below, and Northeast Harbor and the offshore Cranberry Islands beyond. Both peaks also offer good views of the larger mountains to the west, including Norumbega.

A trail descending the south side of Bald Peak allows hikers to avoid backtracking. It reaches a carriage road after 0.4 mile. Head right and take the carriage road that bears left ahead to return to your car for a 2-mile hike.

MAP 12: PARKMAN & CEDAR SWAMP MTNS.

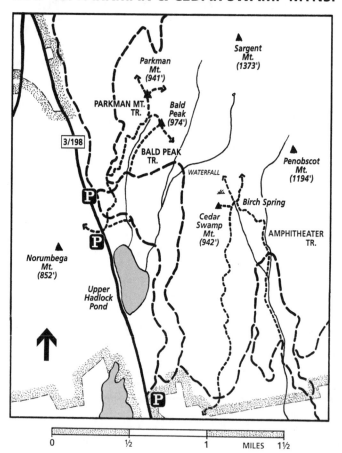

Sargent Mt. (1373')

Parkman Mt. (941')

PARKMAN MT. TR.

Bald Peak (974')

BALD PEAK TR.

Penobscot Mt. (1194')

3/198

WATERFALL

Birch Spring

Cedar Swamp Mt. (942')

AMPHITHEATER TR.

Norumbega Mt. (852')

Upper Hadlock Pond

0   ½   1   MILES   1½

Cedar Swamp Mountain   *(Strenuous)*

With one of the gentlest gradients of any of Mount Desert Island's major summits, Cedar Swamp Mountain is a very enjoyable, albeit long, walk of almost 4 miles. Avoiding backtracking, however, involves a bit more scrambling.

Park at the Brown Mountain Gatehouse lot on Route 198 just above Northeast Harbor. Take the carriage road to the right and then go right again at the intersection, where the trail crosses the carriage road about 0.75 mile from the start.

Turn left onto the trail and begin a gradual ascent over ledges and through fragrant forest. After about 0.5 mile, views begin to open up to the east and west. Farther along, open ledges and areas of low, shrubby vegetation make views even better. Just before reaching the top, the trail skirts cliffs on the east overlooking a high-sided valley known as the Amphitheater. When you reach high ground, a side trail leads several yards to the actual summit post.

The main trail descends steeply though medium-sized boulders to the narrow valley between Cedar Swamp Mountain and Penobscot Mountain. Just downhill from a four-way intersection is Birch Spring, which has reliable water for most of the year.

The cedar swamp for which the mountain is named is actually located farther north in this narrow valley. It is unusual to find such a wet, grassy area so high. It is worth a quick side trip.

Retrace your steps, or take a right at Birch Spring and take the Amphitheater Trail down into the bowl. Turning right again when you hit the carriage road will head you back to the parking area. Leave plenty of time to check out the magnificent stone arch bridge on the carriage road.

Distance to the summit is 1.75 miles. Total distance for the longer trip is just under 4 miles.

13. West of Somes Sound

Acadia Mountain   *(Moderate)*

Overlooking the west shore of Somes Sound, Acadia Mountain offers rewards beyond what its modest 681-foot summit might suggest. The 0.5-mile trail to the second and lower summit has several steep sections, but is easy enough to be included on the list of guided walks offered by the National Park Service. The toughest section is the 0.25-mile descent from the ridge south to the end of the Man o' War Brook Fire Road. This can be avoided by simply retracing your steps.

Park on the west side of Route 102 in the well-marked Acadia Mountain parking area. The trail begins directly across the road. It heads north for a short way before crossing the fire road and turning to the northeast. It rises steadily, with several steep sections, before mounting the relatively flat summit, punctuated by gnarly jack pines. At the summit and farther along, at a lower part of the ridge to the east, views are excellent.

To avoid backtracking, descend a very steep trail to the fire road. Be sure to take a short side trip to see where Man o' War Brook empties into the sound. The brook got its name from the Revolutionary-era warships that would use the waterfall at the end of the brook to fill their water casks.

Turn right on the fire road for a long, yet steady uphill climb back to Route 102, for a total trip of just under 2 miles (slightly less if you choose to backtrack).

During the hotter months, be sure to bring your swimsuit. A trail leads downhill from the parking area to a popular swimming ledge on Echo Lake. No lifeguards are on duty, as the ledges are not an official park service beach.

MAP 13: WEST OF SOMES SOUND

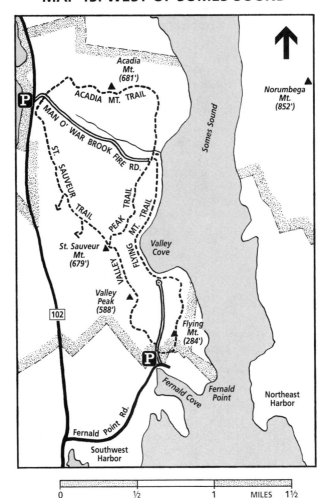

Acadia
Mt.
(681')

ACADIA MT. TRAIL

Norumbega
Mt.
(852')

MAN O' WAR BROOK FIRE RD.

ST. SAUVEUR TRAIL

PEAK TRAIL

FLYING MT. TRAIL

Somes Sound

P

St. Sauveur
Mt.
(679')

VALLEY

Valley
Cove

Valley
Peak
(588')

102

Flying
Mt.
(284')

P

Fernald
Cove

Fernald Point

Northeast
Harbor

Fernald Point Rd.

Southwest
Harbor

0   ½   1   MILES   1½

St. Sauveur Mountain   (Moderate)

Those wishing to hike up 679-foot St. Sauveur Mountain have several options. The most gradual ascent begins at the Acadia Mountain parking area on Route 102. Cross the road and take the trail that heads right and rises gradually toward the summit. Numerous open ledges and stands of jack pines will be encountered. While not as flat and open as some, the summit, reached in a mile, has splendid views in all directions. Take the trail that heads north and descends steeply into the Man o' War Brook valley. Notice how the vegetation and terrain change on this darker and damper side of the mountain. Turn left on the fire road to return (see the Acadia Mountain directions). This route covers 2.25 miles.

Another option is to continue southeast from the summit, descending to Valley Peak. This trail, which has some very steep sections, continues to the Valley Cove Road about 0.75 mile from the summit. Turn left and stroll down the gradual incline to a cove surrounded by impressive cliffs. A trail leads west and then north along the cove and connects up with the fire road. Return to the parking area for a total trip of about 3.75 miles.

Flying Mountain   (Moderate)

You can't honestly say you've climbed them all on Mount Desert Island until you have topped the often overlooked Flying Mountain in Southwest Harbor.

Turn off Route 102 onto Fernald Point Road where you see the signs for the Causeway Club Golf Course. About a mile down the road, at the end of Fernald Cove, park at the gated dirt road on the left. The trail starts on the right 200 yards ahead. It rises steeply to the treed, yet open, summit in less than 0.5 mile.

At only 284 feet, Flying Mountain is no Everest, but it offers stunning views north up Somes Sound (the only true fjord on the east coast of North America), east toward Northeast Harbor, and south out over the Great Harbor of Mount Desert. Immediately below, on Fernald Point, is the site of the first attempted settlement on Mount Desert Island. A party of 40 or so French Jesuits under the direction of Father Pierre Baird settled there in 1613. Their glee at finding such a verdant place to settle was destroyed some four weeks later, when an English warship, tipped off by Indians, attacked the colony and sent them packing.

Retrace your steps or take the trail to the north, which leads down across the talus slopes to the shore of Valley Cove. Take a left on the dirt road in the valley. This will return you to the starting point. The complete loop (using the northern trail) is 1 mile.

14. Ship Harbor
and Wonderland

The late Mount Desert naturalist and renowned birder Ralph Long called the woods and shores around Wonderland and Ship Harbor one of the best birding areas in the state of Maine.

Ship Harbor Nature Trail *(Easy)*

The Ship Harbor Trail is an easy and fun walk for the entire family, and an ideal first trip to acquaint visitors with some of the ecology of Mount Desert Island. Booklets to help explain stops along the self-guided trail are available at Acadia National Park headquarters in Bar Harbor, the nearby Seawall Campground, and area stores.

According to famed historian Samuel Eliot Morison, the harbor got its name after a local vessel, pursued by an English man o' war, sought refuge in the inlet and ran aground during the Revolution.

Starting from the well-marked parking area along State Route 102A, the trail is an elongated figure eight. Direction of travel is merely a matter of personal preference. Signs help to explain environmental processes and identify trees and lichens.

As the trail reaches the ocean, look to the east to spot Long Ledge, which was the scene of a tragic mystery in the winter of 1739–40. The sailing vessel Grand Design approached Ship Harbor, mistaking it for the mouth of a river. It struck the ledge, and the wreck, coupled with the cold and minimal provisions, left few survivors, who were rescued months later after subsisting on clams and native plants. Immediately after the wreck, some of the settlers and crew set out for the settlement at Warren, more than 100 miles to the west, and were never heard from again.

The 1.5-mile Ship Harbor Nature Trail is an easy walk with a few medium grades, and is an excellent place to spend an afternoon discovering some of the secrets of Acadia's forests and shores.

MAP 14: SHIP HARBOR & WONDERLAND

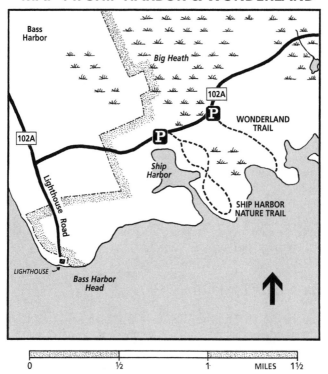

Wonderland Trail *(Easy)*

Slightly closer to the Seawall Campground on Route 102A is the parking area and trailhead for the Wonderland Trail. This 0.5-mile point-to-point walk (1-mile-plus round trip) on a wide, mostly level path features only a modest elevation gain as it tops a 60-foot hill midway in your journey. The walk begins in mixed woods and ends in a grove of spruce along the shore overlooking a peninsula with a pretty pebble beach and granite ledges.

15. Beech Mountain and Canada Cliff

Beech Mountain   *(Strenuous)*

With its distinctive fire tower, Beech Mountain, at 839 feet, is a popular hiking destination. The fire tower, although it is sometimes staffed by interpretive personnel in summer, is closed and used for fire spotting only during extremely dangerous fire conditions.

Most visitors park in the Beech Mountain lot, nestled between the east and west peaks. It is only a short walk west to the summit on the Beech Mountain Trail: 0.5 mile of steady ascent, with hikers deciding which of two branches to actually use to reach the top.

Two other trails that start on park fire roads near the end of Long Pond in Southwest Harbor offer pleasant walks through lush forests, although distances and elevation gains are greater.

Canada Cliff Trail   *(Ladder)*

Beginning at the Echo Lake Beach parking area, the Canada Cliff Trail is one of the most physically challenging on the island. Numerous wooden handrails, tall iron ladders, and the occasional iron railing are used to aid hikers in their ascent. This is not a trail for anyone who has a fear of heights.

The trail switchbacks up the cliff before reaching the top of the eastern peak of Beech Mountain in 0.5 mile. Hikers can do a short loop overlooking scenic Echo Lake, or continue down a short, steep grade down to the summit parking area, where they can catch the Beech Mountain Trail to the fire tower.

MAP 15: BEECH MTN. & CANADA CLIFF

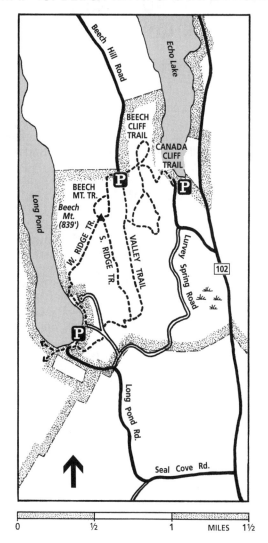

16. Western Mountain and Seal Cove Marsh

Western Mountain

Western Mountain is actually three distinct peaks, including Bernard Mountain to the west, Knight Nubble in the center, and Mansell Mountain, overlooking Long Pond to the east. Together, this trio offers a wonderful lengthy hike (4.75 miles) over three distinct wooded summits. Individually, each offers great opportunities for half-day trips.

Bernard Mountain   *(Strenuous)*

This trip begins at the gravel parking area off the Western Mountain Road. The South Face Trail rises gradually through thick forest on the remains of an old logging road, signs of which soon disappear. The first views to the west begin to appear after 0.5 mile. Short, unmarked side trails lead to ledge overlooks.

As the trail approaches the summit, it passes through some of the only old-growth forest remaining on Mount Desert Island. The open coniferous woods have an ethereal appearance. At about 1.3 miles, a wooden post marks where the newly opened West Face Trail, which begins on the Western Mountain Road near Seal Cove Pond, connects from the west. The trail levels out for a short distance before reaching the 1071-foot summit, almost hidden in the trees. A little farther along is an open area with a log bench and wonderful views to the north. Total trip is 1.8 miles.

To return, continue down a very steep descent into the col between Bernard and Knight Nubble. A right here onto the Sluiceway Trail will take you past a small fire reservoir at the mountain's base and return you to your vehicle.

Knight Nubble   *(Strenuous)*

To continue across the Western Mountain ridge, do not turn at the Sluiceway Trail, but ascend steeply to the top of Knight Nubble.

MAP 16: WESTERN MTN. & SEAL COVE MARSH

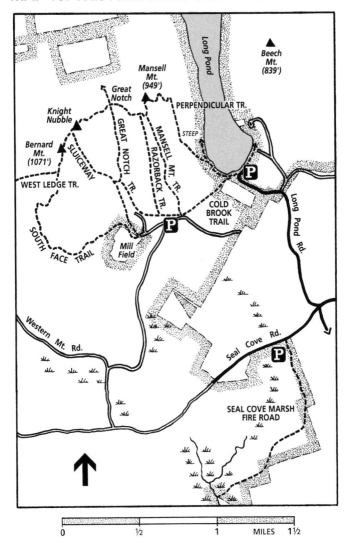

Long Pond

Beech
Mt.
(839')

Mansell
Mt.
(949')

Great
Notch

PERPENDICULAR TR.

Knight
Nubble

STEEP

Bernard
Mt.
(1071')

GREAT NOTCH TR.

MANSELL MT. TR.

RAZORBACK TR.

SLUICEWAY

WEST LEDGE TR.

P

P

COLD
BROOK
TRAIL

Long Pond Rd.

SOUTH FACE TRAIL

Mill
Field

Western Mt. Rd.

Seal Cove Rd.

P

SEAL COVE MARSH
FIRE ROAD

0   ½   1   MILES   1½

At last inspection there was no summit marker. Just beyond the top there is a good ledge overlook to the southeast.

The trail continues to descend and then levels off through a thick wood. One more major steep descent puts you at the bottom of the Great Notch. A hiker's journal kept in a box fastened to a tree, and some log benches, make the Great Notch an attractive place to pause. A right turn here will return you to the mountain's base.

The trail leading north from this intersection splits, with one branch ending on the Seal Cove Fire Road and the other curving out around Mansell Mountain to skirt the edge of Long Pond.

Mansell Mountain   *(Strenuous)*

Rising again, the trail heads for the 949-foot summit of Mansell Mountain, passing over a series of distinct north–south humps. The terrain is a mix of open ledges and forest glens. You will pass several steep trails leading down off the mountain. After cutting north, the trail reaches the unremarkable summit a total of 3 miles from the start of the Western Mountain route.

Don't waste time here, but continue for another 0.25 mile to the wide-open ledges that overlook Long Pond. This is the best view Mansell has to offer.

To descend, take the Perpendicular Trail *(Ladder)*. It starts by following a seasonal stream course and then runs along the base of smooth granite cliffs. Several sections are very steep, with numerous stone steps. There are several iron rungs and one short ladder to negotiate.

Take a right when you reach the trail along the lake. Turn right again just before reaching the pumphouse and stroll back to Mill Field along the gently undulating Cold Brook Trail as it passes through pretty woods.

The full-length round trip is 4.75 miles.

Seal Cove Marsh Fire Road   *(Easy)*

Seldom visited by anyone, the smooth gravel Seal Cove Marsh Fire Road makes for a pleasant afternoon's stroll through some of the wildest country in Acadia. Park carefully off to the left side of the Seal Cove Road 0.4 mile west of the intersection with the Long Pond Road. The entrance to the fire road is overgrown, set back a ways, and not easy to spot. Be sure not to block the gate.

The road heads south, and then more west, climbing up and down over several low hills. Marshy cedar swamps alternate with pretty stretches of open woodland. Keep a careful eye out for the tracks and sign of white-tailed deer and coyotes. Enjoy the quiet forest and try to practice identifying birds by their songs.

After 1.5 miles the road ends at the backwater stream that leads to the tidal Bass Harbor Marsh. Reverse your direction to return.

Books of Interest

David L. Kendall, *Glaciers and Granite: A Guide to Maine's Landscape and Geology* (Belfast, Me.: North Country Press) 1987.

Gladys O'Neil and G. W. Helfrich, *Lost Bar Harbor* (Camden. Me.: Down East Books) 1986.

Ann Rockefeller Roberts, *Mr. Rockefeller's Roads: The Untold Story of Acadia's Carriage Roads and their Creator* (Camden. Me.: Down East Books) 1990.

Diana Abrell, *A Pocket Guide to Carriage Roads of Acadia National Park,* 2nd edition (Camden. Me.: Down East Books) 1995.

William V. P. Newlin, *The Down East Guide to the Lakes and Ponds of Mt. Desert* (Camden. Me.: Down East Books) 1988.

George B. Dorr, *Acadia National Park, Its Origin and Background* (Bangor, Me.: Acadia Press) 1942.

Sargent F. Collier, *Mt. Desert Island and Acadia National Park* (Camden. Me.: Down East Books) 1978.

Tom St. Germain and Jay Saunders, *Trails of History: The Story of Mount Desert Island's Paths from Norumbega to Acadia* (Bar Harbor, Me.: Parkman Publications) 1993.

Robert Rothe, *Acadia: The Story Behind the Scenery* (Las Vegas: KC Publications) 1981.

Freeman Tilden, *The National Parks* (New York: Knopf) 1968.

Samuel Eliot Morison, *The Story of Mount Desert Island* (Boston: Little Brown) 1959.

Dale Rex Coman, *The Native Mammals, Reptiles, and Amphibians of Mount Desert Island* (Bar Harbor: Acadia Publishing) 1981.

Ruth Gortner Grierson, *Nature Diary of Mount Desert Island* (Mt. Desert, Me.: Windswept House) 1993.

Ralph H. Long, *Native Birds of Mount Desert Island and Acadia National Park* (Privately published) 1987.

Index of Hikes and Trails

The Mt. Desert Island Pocket Guide Outdoor Series

PUBLISHED BY DOWN EAST BOOKS

A Pocket Guide to Biking on Mount Desert Island
By Audrey Shelton Minutolo
18 selected loop routes, ranging from all-day
circuits to shorter routes designed for families with
small children, are accompanied by maps,
photographs, and tips.

*A Pocket Guide to Paddling the Waters
of Mount Desert Island*
By Earl Brechlin
In sections covering creeks, wetlands, ponds, and
saltwater, 18 different canoe and kayak routes are described
along with helpful information, maps, and photographs.

*A Pocket Guide to the Carriage Roads
of Acadia National Park, Second Edition*
By Diana F. Abrell
This perennially popular guide to Acadia's 51-mile
carriage road network includes new information for
hikers, skiers, horseback riders, and bicyclists. 12 maps.
